Digging into the Past

by Damian Harvey
Illustrated by Srimalie Bassani

Contents

Clues to the Past 2
Maps and Objects 6
Going Underground 10
Careful Work 14
Hidden Treasure 18
After the Dig 22
Glossary and Index 24

adult

Clues to the Past

We can find out about life in the past by carefully examining the places where people used to live. A person who studies objects and buildings from long ago is called an archaeologist.

However, you don't have to be an archaeologist to find out secrets from the past! You just have to look carefully around you.

child

In the present this is my home, but in the past it was a field. It looked so different!

The present means right now. What is in the picture in the present that wouldn't have been there in the past, when it was a field?

child

I want to find lots of things from the past. What places could I look in?

adult

Maps and Objects

It's easy to spot some big buildings from the past, like castles. However, you can also use maps to see where old buildings used to be.

Aerial photographs can also help us discover buildings from the past. Walls under the ground can show up as shapes.

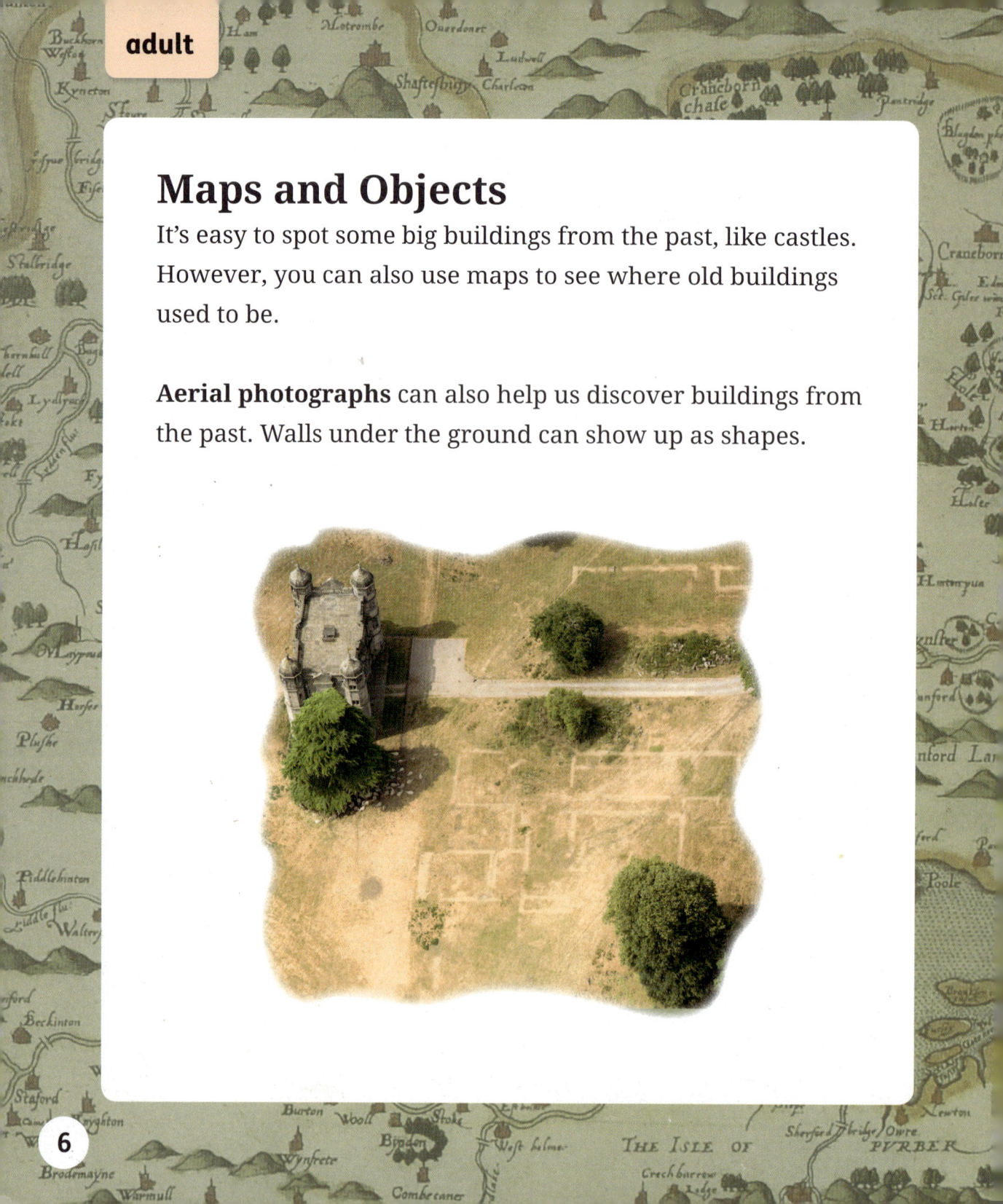

child

This seat in the park is odd. It is a stone circle with a hole in it.

child

This old map shows that a windmill stood here in the past. The stone came from the windmill. It is called a millstone.

child

The windmill made the stone turn around to **grind** corn into flour.

In the stone's centre is a hole where the corn was put so the mill would grind it. Can you point to the stone's centre? Can you point to the centre of the room we're in?

adult

Going Underground

Over hundreds of years, layers of rubbish and soil can cover up things that are on the ground. Archaeologists have to dig down to find them.

First, archaeologists dig narrow 'test pits' to find the best places. Then they begin to remove layers of soil using special tools.

child

Experts use tools like these to find things that are hidden underground.

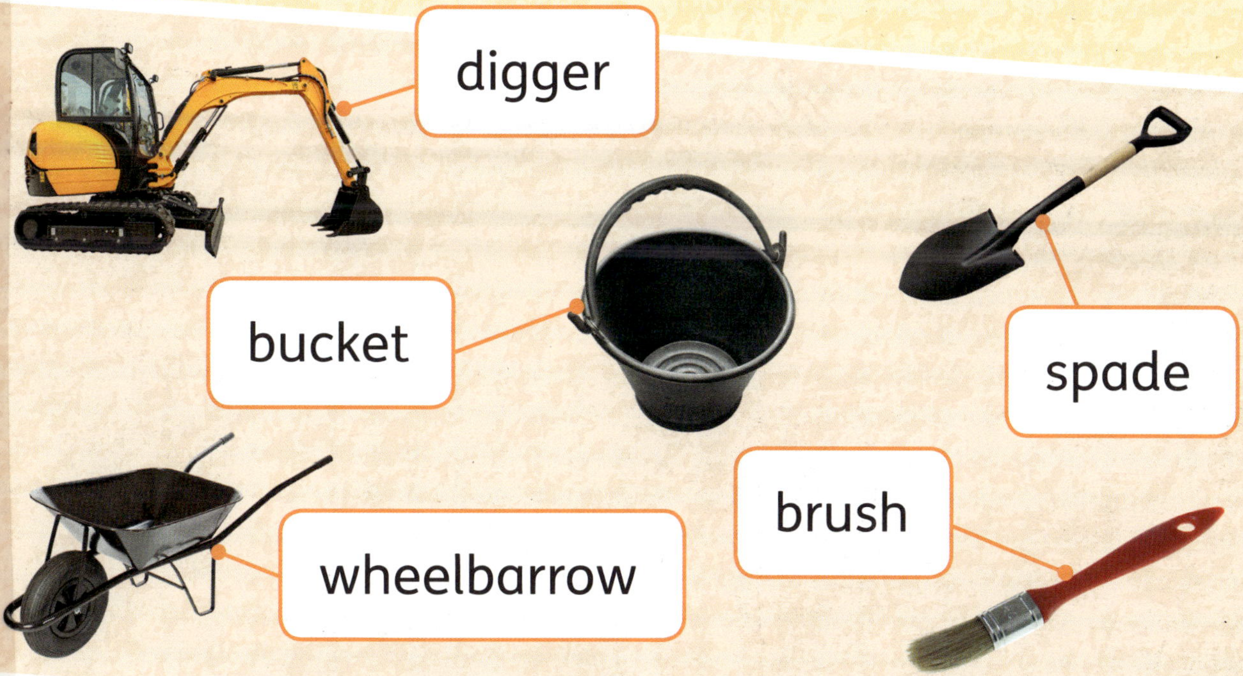

- digger
- bucket
- spade
- wheelbarrow
- brush

child

The experts use spades to dig out soil.
They have found a row of stones.
These might be part of a **Roman villa**.

child

Can you see bits of an old bowl?
The experts can tell it is **Roman**.

adult

Careful Work

The archaeologists have to be very careful when they are digging. They do not want to damage anything. First they use diggers, then spades, then brushes as they dig deeper.

child

They use little brushes to clean away the rest of the soil. It is a slow job!

child

They need to wash the bits of pots to show all the details.

child

Can you see some black and white tiles making a pattern? An artist made this in the <u>distant</u> past.

If something comes from the <u>distant</u> past, was it made a very long time ago, or not so long ago?

adult

Hidden Treasure

The pattern is a mosaic! Rich Romans often had mosaics on their floors. They were made up of thousands of tiny coloured pieces called 'tesserae' (*say* tess-er-eye), arranged to make beautiful pictures.

child

It takes a lot of brushing and cleaning to reveal a <u>narrow</u> bit of the pattern.

Something that is <u>narrow</u> is not wide. Can you find something <u>narrow</u> in the room right now?

child

Now that the tiles are clean, you can see human shapes.

child

The pots and tiles tell the experts a lot about life in the past.

The things archaeologists find give them information about the past. What new information have you found out from reading this book?

adult

After the Dig

Sometimes when the digging is over, the archaeologists have to put back all of the soil and make sure everywhere is left neat and tidy. This also helps to protect the delicate things that have been found.

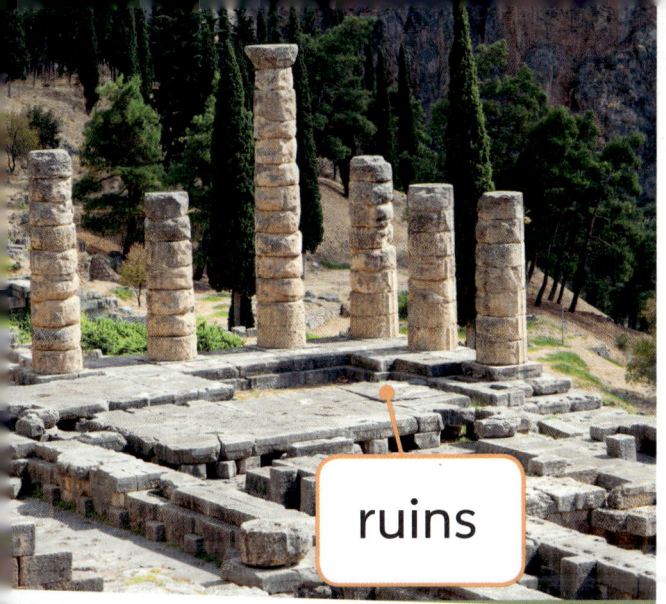
ruins

child

Some **ruins** and objects from the past are put on show in different places for people to see. They tell us about life in the past!

adult

Glossary

aerial photographs: pictures taken from high in the air
grind: crush into tiny, smooth pieces
Roman: made by the ancient Roman people
Roman villa: large fancy house from Roman times
ruins: buildings which have fallen down

Index

coin 3
millstone 8, 9
mosaic 17–20
tools 10–11, 12, 14–15
Romans 12, 13, 18

Throughout the book there are words in **bold**. We can use the Glossary together to look up what these words mean. The Index will help us find key information.